HIDE & SPEAK
CHINESE

Catherine Bruzzone and Susan Martineau
Chinese text: 郭力明 Liming Guo Barrett
Illustrated by Louise Comfort

BARRON'S

农场上 nóng chǎng shàng - On the farm

1 猫在追老鼠。**māo** zài zhuī **lǎo shǔ**

2 狗在太阳下睡觉。**gǒu** zài tài yáng xià shuì jiào

3 马在马厩里。**mǎ** zài mǎ jiù lǐ

4 牛的旁边有一桶牛奶。**niú** de páng biān yǒu yī tǒng niú nǎi

5 猪在吃很多东西！**zhū** zài chī hěn duō dōng xi

6 羊在田里。**yáng** zài tián lǐ

7 鸭子在池塘里游水。**yā zi** zài chí táng lǐ yóu shuǐ

8 山羊在吃草。**shān yáng** zài chī cǎo

1 **The cat** is chasing **the mouse**.

2 **The dog** is sleeping in the sun.

3 **The horse** is in the stable.

4 There is a bucket of milk beside **the cow.**

5 **The pig** is eating a lot!

6 **The sheep** are in the field.

7 **The duck** is swimming on the pond.

8 **The goat** is eating grass.

猫
māo

老 鼠
lǎo shǔ

狗
gǒu

马
mǎ

牛
niú

猪
zhū

羊
yáng

鸭 子
yā zi

山羊
shān yáng

教室里 jiào shì lǐ - *In the classroom*

1 **老师说:**"请安静!" **lǎo shī** shuō: "qǐng ān jìng!"	1 ***The teacher*** says "Silence!"
2 芭芭拉在**椅子**上。bā bā lā zài **yǐ zi** shàng	2 *Barbara is on **the chair**.*
3 皮特在**桌子**下。pí tè zài **zhuō zi** xià	3 *Peter is under **the table**.*
4 马修在扔**书**。mǎ xiū zài rēng **shū**	4 *Matthew is throwing **the book**.*
5 伊丽莎白在用**彩色铅笔**涂画。 yī lì shā bái zài yòng **cǎi sè qiān bǐ** tú huà	5 *Elizabeth is scribbling with **the color pencils**.*
6 罗伯特把**胶水**掉了。luó bó tè bǎ **jiāo shuǐ** diào le	6 *Robert drops **the glue**.*
7 玛丽在剪**纸**。mǎ lì zài jiǎn **zhǐ**	7 *Mary is cutting up **the paper**.*
8 **钢笔**在**桌子**上。**gāng bǐ** zài **zhuō zi** shàng	8 ***The pen*** is on **the table**.
9 保罗在静静地玩**电脑**! bǎo luó zài jìng jìng de wán **diàn nǎo**	9 *And Paul is playing quietly with **the computer**!*

	老师 lǎo shī
	椅子 yǐ zi
	桌子 zhuō zi
	书 shū
	彩色铅笔 cǎi sè qiān bǐ
	胶水 jiāo shuǐ
	纸 zhǐ
	钢笔 gāng bǐ
	电脑 diàn nǎo

摸摸你的头 mō mō nǐ de tóu - Touch your head

1 我摸我的**头**。 wǒ mō wǒ de **tóu**

2 我摸我的**眼睛**。 wǒ mō wǒ de **yǎn jīng**

3 我摸我的**鼻子**。 wǒ mō wǒ de **bí zi**

4 我摸我的**嘴**。 wǒ mō wǒ de **zuǐ**

5 我摸我的**肩膀**。 wǒ mō wǒ de **jiān bǎng**

6 我摸我的**胳膊**。 wǒ mō wǒ de **gē bo**

7 我摸我的**手**。 wǒ mō wǒ de **shǒu**

8 我摸我的**腿**。 wǒ mō wǒ de **tuǐ**

9 我摸我的**脚**。 wǒ mō wǒ de **jiǎo**

1 I'm touching **my head**.

2 I'm touching **my eyes**.

3 I'm touching **my nose**.

4 I'm touching **my mouth**.

5 I'm touching **my shoulders**.

6 I'm touching **my arm**.

7 I'm touching **my hand**.

8 I'm touching **my leg**.

9 I'm touching **my foot**.

头
tóu

眼睛
yǎn jīng

鼻子
bí zi

嘴
zuǐ

肩膀
jiān bǎng

胳膊
gē bo

手
shǒu

腿
tuǐ

脚
jiǎo

丛林里 cóng lín lǐ - In the jungle

1	红色的瓢虫	hóng sè de piáo chóng	1	a **red** ladybug
2	蓝色的蝴蝶	lán sè de hú dié	2	a **blue** butterfly
3	绿色的叶子	lǜ sè de yè zi	3	a **green** leaf
4	黄色的水果	huáng sè de shuǐ guǒ	4	a **yellow** fruit
5	橙色的鹦鹉	chéng sè de yīng wǔ	5	an **orange** parrot
6	黑色的蚂蚁	hēi sè de mǎ yǐ	6	a **black** ant
7	白色的蝴蝶	bái sè de hú dié	7	a **white** butterfly
8	紫色的鲜花	zǐ sè de xiān huā	8	a **purple** flower
9	棕色的树枝	zōng sè de shù zhī	9	a **brown** branch

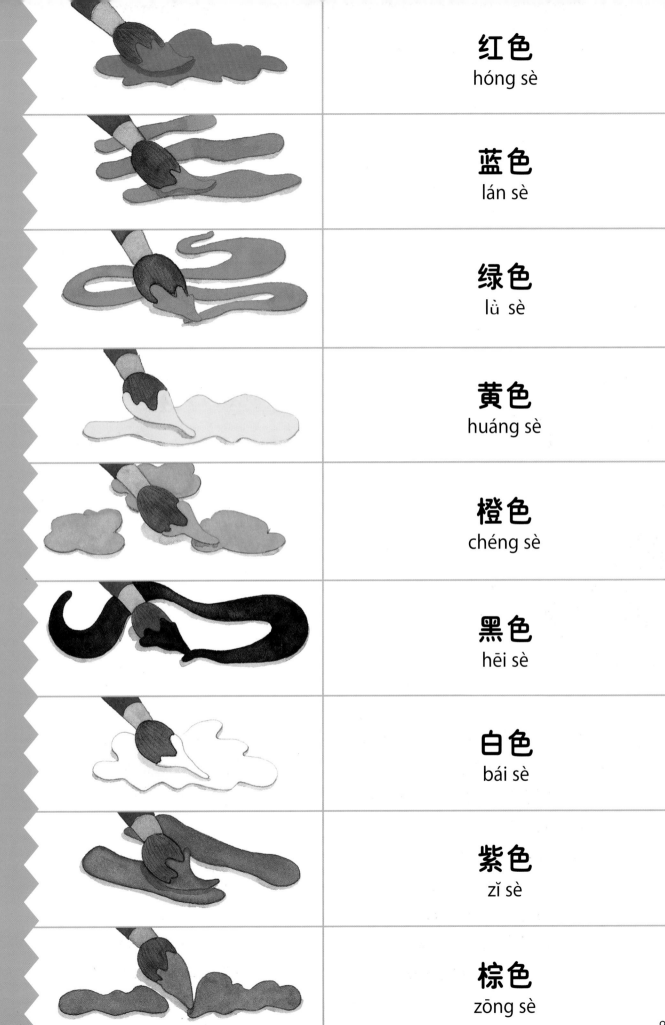

颜色 yán sè - Colors

红色
hóng sè

蓝色
lán sè

绿色
lǜ sè

黄色
huáng sè

橙色
chéng sè

黑色
hēi sè

白色
bái sè

紫色
zǐ sè

棕色
zōng sè

道具箱 dào jù xiāng - The dressing-up chest

1	我在穿**裙子**。wǒ zài chuān **qún zi**	1	I'm putting on **the skirt**.
2	你在穿**连衣裙**吗？nǐ zài chuān **lián yī qún** ma	2	Are you putting on **the dress**?
3	卡罗琳在穿**裤子**。kǎ luó lín zài chuān **kù zi**	3	Caroline is putting on **the pants**.
4	詹姆士在穿**大衣**。zhān mǔ shì zài chuān **dà yī**	4	James is putting on **the coat**.
5	我们在穿**鞋**。wǒ men zài chuān **xié**	5	We're putting on **the shoes**.
6	约翰和杰克在穿**衬衣**。yuē hàn hé jié kè zài chuān **chèn yī**	6	John and Jack are putting on **the shirt**.
7	露西在穿**睡衣**。lù xī zài chuān **shuì yī**	7	Lucy is putting on **the pajamas**.
8	小宝宝在穿**袜子**。xiǎo bǎo bǎo zài chuān **wà zi**	8	The baby is putting on **the socks**.
9	小狗在戴**帽子**。xiǎo gǒu zài dài **mào zi**	9	The dog is putting on **the hat**.

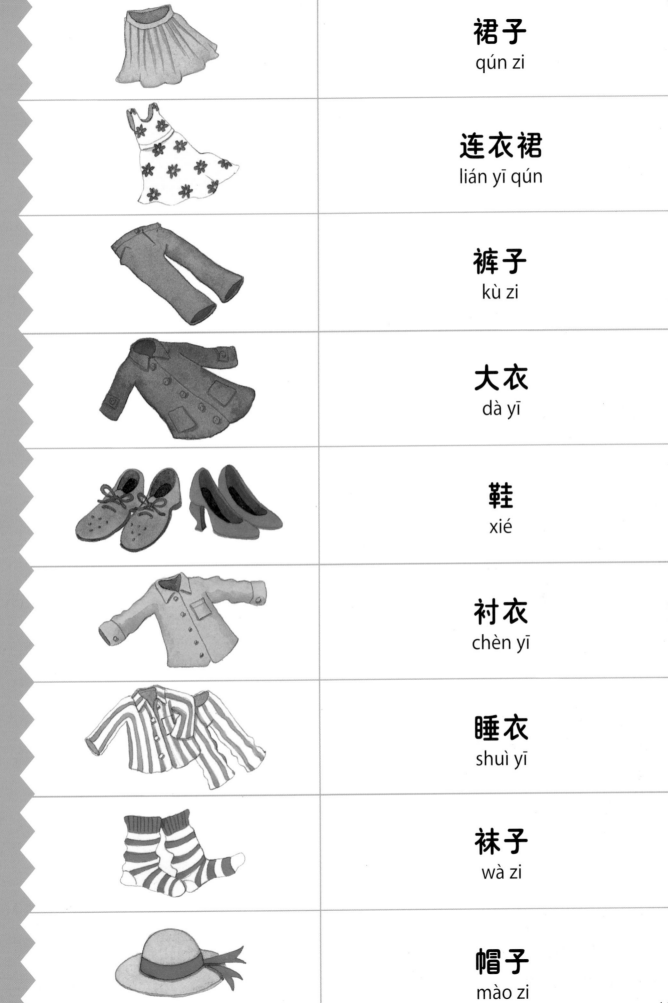

裙子
qún zi

连衣裙
lián yī qún

裤子
kù zi

大衣
dà yī

鞋
xié

衬衣
chèn yī

睡衣
shuì yī

袜子
wà zi

帽子
mào zi

动物园里 dòng wù yuán lǐ - At the zoo

1	**长颈鹿**有一个小宝宝。 **cháng jǐng lù** yǒu yī gè xiǎo bǎo bǎo	1	**The giraffe** has a baby.
2	**狮子**在大树下睡觉。 **shī zi** zài dà shù xià shuì jiào	2	**The lion** is sleeping under the tree.
3	**老虎**在吃食。 **lǎo hǔ** zài chī shí	3	**The tiger** is eating its meal.
4	**大象**在洗澡。 **dà xiàng** zài xǐ zǎo	4	**The elephant** is washing.
5	**鳄鱼**在湖里游泳。 **è yú** zài hú lǐ yóu yǒng	5	**The crocodile** is swimming in the lake.
6	**蛇**在大树上。 **shé** zài dà shù shàng	6	**The snake** is in the tree.
7	**北极熊**在爬岩石。 **běi jí xióng** zài pá yán shí	7	**The polar bear** is climbing on a rock.
8	**河马**喜欢在泥里玩。 **hé mǎ** xǐ huān zài ní lǐ wán	8	**The hippopotamus** likes mud.
9	**海豚**一跃到空中。 **hǎi tún** yī yuè dào kōng zhōng	9	**The dolphin** is jumping in the air.

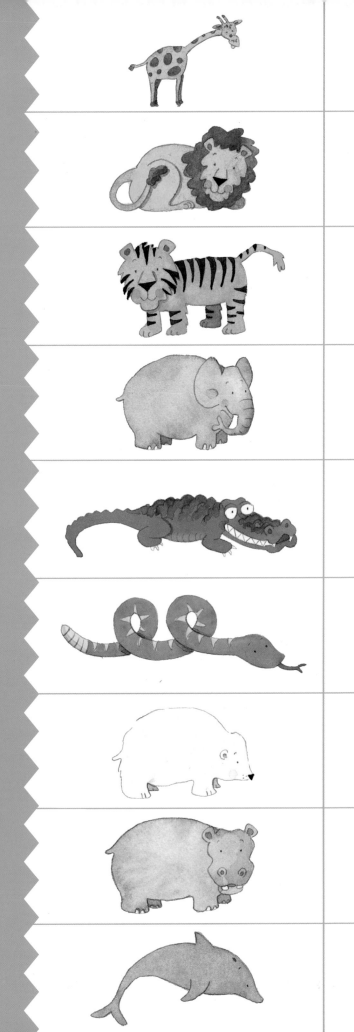

	长颈鹿 cháng jǐng lù
	狮子 shī zi
	老虎 lǎo hǔ
	大象 dà xiàng
	鳄鱼 è yú
	蛇 shé
	北极熊 běi jí xióng
	河马 hé mǎ
	海豚 hǎi tún

街道上 jiē dào shàng - On the street

1	女士在过**街道**。nǚ shì zài guò **jiē dào**	1	The woman is crossing **the street**.
2	孩子们在**行人道**上。hái zi men zài **xíng rén dào** shàng	2	The children are on **the sidewalk**.
3	**公共汽车**停在**公共汽车站**。**gōng gòng qì chē** tíng zài **gōng gòng qì chē zhàn**	3	**The bus** stops at **the bus stop**.
4	**货车**停在**红绿灯**前。**huò chē** tíng zài **hóng lǜ dēng** qián	4	**The truck** stops at **the traffic lights**.
5	男孩子在骑**自行车**。nán hái zi zài qí **zì xíng chē**	5	The boy is on **the bicycle**.
6	**小汽车**是红色的。**xiǎo qì chē** shì hóng sè de	6	**The car** is red.
7	**警车**开得很快。**jǐng chē** kāi dé hěn kuài	7	**The police car** is going fast.

	街道 jiē dào
	行人道 xíng rén dào
	公共汽车 gōng gòng qì chē
	公共汽车站 gōng gòng qì chē zhàn
	货车 huò chē
	红绿灯 hóng lǜ dēng
	自行车 zì xíng chē
	小汽车 xiǎo qì chē
	警车 jǐng chē

沙滩上 shā tān shàng - At the beach

1 **大海**是蓝色的。 **dà hǎi** shì lán sè de
2 **沙**是黄色的。 **shā** shì huáng sè de
3 **海鸥**在吃**鱼**。 **hǎi ōu** zài chī **yú**
4 **海草**是绿色的。 **hǎi cǎo** shì lǜ sè de
5 **贝壳**在**岩石**上。 **bèi ké** zài **yán shí** shàng
6 孩子们在**帆船**里。 hái zi men zài **fān chuán** lǐ
7 海上有很多大**浪**。 hǎi shàng yǒu hěn duō dà **làng**

1 **The sea** is blue.
2 **The sand** is yellow.
3 **The seagull** is eating **the fish**.
4 **The seaweed** is green.
5 **The shell** is on **the rock**.
6 The children are in **the sailboat**.
7 There are many big **waves**.

大海
dà hǎi

沙
shā

海鸥
hǎi ōu

鱼
yú

海草
hǎi cǎo

贝壳
bèi ké

岩石
yán shí

帆船
fān chuán

浪
làng

我的一家 wǒ de yì jiā - My family

1 我**妈妈**坐在桌子旁边。
wǒ **mā ma** zuò zài zhuō zi páng biān

2 我**爸爸**和我**爷爷**在说话。
wǒ **bà ba** hé wǒ **yé ye** zài shuō huà

3 我**弟弟**在玩他的小火车。
wǒ **dì di** zài wán tā de xiǎo huǒ chē

4 我**奶奶**在吃意大利面。
wǒ **nǎi nai** zài chī yì dà lì miàn

5 我**阿姨**在帮助我**妹妹**。
wǒ **ā yí** zài bāng zhù wǒ **mèi mei**

6 我**叔叔**在喝水。 wǒ **shū shu** zài hē shuǐ

7 **孩子们**在看电视。
hái zi men zài kàn diàn shì

1 **My mother** is sitting at the table.

2 **My father** is talking to **my grandfather**.

3 **My brother** is playing with his train.

4 **My grandmother** is eating spaghetti.

5 **My aunt** is helping **my sister**.

6 **My uncle** is drinking some water.

7 **The children** are watching television.

妈妈
mā ma

爸爸
bà ba

姐姐(elder sister)/**妹妹**(younger sister)
jiě jie/mèi mei

哥哥(elder brother)/**弟弟**(younger brother)
gē ge/dì di

奶奶(father's side)/**外婆**(mother's side)
nǎi nai/wài pó

爷爷(father's side)/**外公**(mother's side)
yé ye/wài gōng

姑姑(father's side)/**阿姨**(mother's side)
gū gu/ā yí

叔叔(father's side)/**舅舅**(mother's side)
shū shu/jiù jiu

孩子们
hái zi men

开派对！kāi pài duì - Party time!

1	克里斯汀在吃**三明治**。kè lǐ sī tīng zài chī **sān míng zhì**	1	Christine is eating **a sandwich**.
2	小宝宝想要**巧克力**。xiǎo bǎo bǎo xiǎng yào **qiǎo kè lì**	2	The baby wants **some chocolate**.
3	**蛋糕**在桌子上。**dàn gāo** zài zhuō zi shàng	3	**The cake** is on the table.
4	**薯条**很热！**shǔ tiáo** hěn rè	4	**The french fries** are hot!
5	**比萨饼**快吃完了。**bǐ sà bǐng** kuài chī wán le	5	**The pizza** is almost finished.
6	亨利有一个**冰淇淋**。hēng lì yǒu yī gè **bīng qí lín**	6	Henry has **an ice cream**.
7	你想要喝**可乐**还是**橙汁**？nǐ xiǎng yào hē **kě lè** hái shì **chéng zhī**	7	Do you want **soda** or **orange juice**?
8	我更喜欢**水**。wǒ gèng xǐ huān **shuǐ**	8	I prefer **water**.

三明治
sān míng zhì

巧克力
qiǎo kè lì

蛋糕
dàn gāo

薯条
shǔ tiáo

比萨饼
bǐ sà bǐng

冰淇淋
bīng qí lín

可乐
kě lè

橙汁
chéng zhī

水
shuǐ

买玩具 mǎi wán jù - Shopping for toys

1 泰迪熊比男孩子还大。 **tài dí xióng** bǐ nán hái zi hái dà

2 萨拉在和机器人玩。 sà lā zài hé **jī qì rén** wán

3 奥利弗想买那个球。 ào lì fú xiǎng mǎi nà gè **qiú**

4 你更想要拼图还是游戏？ nǐ gèng xiǎng yào **pīn tú** hái shì **yóu xì**

5 台上足球真好玩！ **tái shàng zú qiú** zhēn hǎo wán

6 卡罗和威廉在看电脑游戏。 kǎ luó hé wēi lián zài kàn **diàn nǎo yóu xì**

7 爸爸在买模型飞机。 bà bà zài mǎi **mó xíng fēi jī**

8 女孩子们喜欢串珠。 nǚ hái zi men xǐ huān **chuàn zhū**

1 **The teddy bear** is bigger than the boy.

2 Sarah is playing with **the robot**.

3 Oliver wants to buy **the ball**.

4 Do you prefer **the puzzle** or **the game**?

5 **Table soccer** is really fun!

6 Carol and William are looking at **the computer game**.

7 Dad is buying **the model airplane**.

8 The girls like **the beads**.

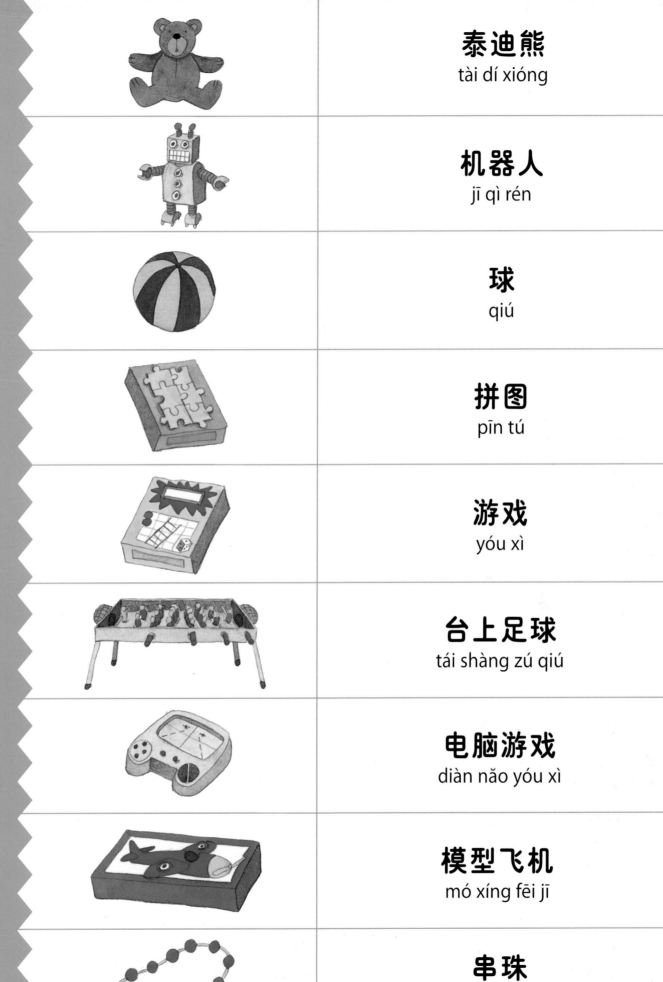

泰迪熊
tài dí xióng

机器人
jī qì rén

球
qiú

拼图
pīn tú

游戏
yóu xì

台上足球
tái shàng zú qiú

电脑游戏
diàn nǎo yóu xì

模型飞机
mó xíng fēi jī

串珠
chuàn zhū

洗碗 xǐ wǎn - Washing dishes

1　爸爸在**洗碗池**里洗碗。bà ba zài **xǐ wǎn chí** lǐ xǐ wǎn

2　妈妈在用**刀**切苹果。mā ma zài yòng **dāo** qiē píng guǒ

3　**勺子**和**叉子**都很脏。**sháo zi** hé **chā zi** dōu hěn zāng

4　朱莉有一**杯**水。zhū lì yǒu yī **bēi** shuǐ

5　小猫在看**冰箱**里的东西！xiǎo māo zài kàn **bīng xiāng** lǐ de dōng xī

6　**盘子**掉了。**pán zi** diào le

7　**平底锅**在**炉灶**上。**píng dǐ guō** zài **lú zào** shàng

1　Daddy is washing dishes in **the sink**.

2　Mommy is cutting the apple with **the knife**.

3　**The spoon** and **the fork** are dirty.

4　Julie has **a glass** of water.

5　The cat is looking in **the fridge**!

6　**The plate** is falling down.

7　**The saucepans** are on **the stove**.

洗碗池
xǐ wǎn chí

刀
dāo

勺子
sháo zi

叉子
chā zi

杯
bēi

冰箱
bīng xiāng

盘子
pán zi

平底锅
píng dǐ guō

炉灶
lú zào

在野外 zài yě wài - In the country

1	海伦在爬树。hǎi lún zài pá **shù**	1	Helen is climbing **the tree**.
2	草地是绿色的。**cǎo dì** shì lǜ sè de	2	**The grass** is green.
3	田野里到处是花。**tián yě** lǐ dào chù shì **huā**	3	**The field** is full of **flowers**.
4	山很高。**shān** hěn gāo	4	**The mountain** is very high.
5	树林里有很多树。**shù lín** lǐ yǒu hěn duō **shù**	5	In **the woods** there are lots of **trees**.
6	桥越过河。**qiáo** yuè guò **hé**	6	**The bridge** crosses **the river**.
7	鸟在筑巢。**niǎo** zài zhù cháo	7	**The bird** is making its nest.

| | 树
shù |
| 草地
cǎo dì |
| 田野
tián yě |
| 花
huā |
| 山
shān |
| 树林
shù lín |
| 桥
qiáo |
| 河
hé |
| 鸟
niǎo |

洗澡 xǐ zǎo - Taking a bath

1　卢克在用**香皂**洗澡。lú kè zài yòng **xiāng zào** xǐ zǎo

2　**洗脸池**里的水很满。**xǐ liǎn chí** lǐ dé shuǐ hěn mǎn

3　丹尼尔在玩**淋浴**。dān ní ěr zài wán **lín yù**

4　猫在**毛巾**上睡觉。māo zài **máo jīn** shàng shuì jiào

5　**马桶**在**浴盆**旁边。**mǎ tǒng** zài **yù pén** páng biān

6　曼德林在把**牙膏**放到**牙刷**上。màn dé lín zài bǎ **yá gāo** fàng dào **yá shuā** shàng

7　**镜子**在**洗脸池**上面。**jìng zi** zài **xǐ liǎn chí** shàng miàn

1　Luke is washing himself with **soap**.

2　**The sink** is full of water.

3　Danny is playing with **the shower**.

4　The cat is sleeping on **the towel**.

5　**The toilet** is next to **the bath**.

6　Madeleine is putting **toothpaste** on **the toothbrush**.

7　**The mirror** is above **the sink**.

香皂
xiāng zào

洗脸池
xǐ liǎn chí

淋浴
lín yù

毛巾
máo jīn

马桶
mǎ tǒng

浴盆
yù pén

牙膏
yá gāo

牙刷
yá shuā

镜子
jìng zi

我的卧室里wǒ de wò shì lǐ - In my bedroom

1	我在我的**床**上睡觉。 wǒ zài wǒ de **chuáng** shàng shuì jiào	1	I'm sleeping in **my bed**.
2	**闹钟**在**书架**上。 **nào zhōng** zài **shū jià** shàng	2	**The alarm clock** is on **the shelf**.
3	我喜欢看**电视**。 wǒ xǐ huān kàn **diàn shì**	3	I like watching **television**.
4	我的**床**在**窗户**旁边。 wǒ de **chuáng** zài **chuāng hu** páng biān	4	**My bed** is near **the window**.
5	我的衣服在**衣柜**里。 wǒ de yī fu zài **yī guì** lǐ	5	My clothes are in **the closet**.
6	我的**随身听**在**地毯**上。 wǒ de **suí shēn tīng** zài **dì tǎn** shàng	6	**My player** is on **the rug**.
7	**妈妈**在开**门**。 **mā ma** zài kāi **mén**	7	Mommy is opening **the door**.